RACIAL JUSTICE IN AMERICA
HISTORIES

ATROCITIES in ACTION

KEVIN P. WINN WITH KELISA WING

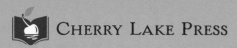
CHERRY LAKE PRESS

Published in the United States of America by Cherry Lake Publishing Group
Ann Arbor, Michigan
www.cherrylakepublishing.com

Reading Adviser: Beth Walker Gambro, MS, Ed., Reading Consultant, Yorkville, IL
Content Adviser: Kelisa Wing
Book Design and Cover Art: Felicia Macheske

Photo Credits: © DiAnna Paulk/Shutterstock, 7; Library of Congress/Photographer unknown, LOC Control No.: 2018670637, 9; Library of Congress/Artwork by Alfred R. Waud, LOC Control No.: 94507780, 10; Library of Congress/Photo by Hart, Watertown, N.Y., [ca. 1870] LOC Control No.: 98519148, 13; Library of Congress/Photo by Underwood & Underwood, LOC Control No.: 2012647922, 14; Schomburg Center for Research in Black Culture, Art and Artifacts Division, The New York Public Library. "KKK (Untitled)" Accessed April 14, 2021. https://digitalcollections.nypl.org/items/f7beb120-c810-0137-5168-75d4a15b3312, 17; © World History Archive / Alamy Stock Photo, 19; © 5D Media/Shutterstock, 20; © Everett Collection Historical / Alamy Stock Photo, 23; © Everett Collection/Shutterstock, 25; © ARCHIVIO GBB / Alamy Stock Photo, 27; © Calvin Stewart/Shutterstock, 28

Graphics Throughout: © debra hughes/Shutterstock.com; © Natewimon Nantiwat/Shutterstock.com

Cherry Lake Press is an imprint of Cherry Lake Publishing Group.

Library of Congress Cataloging-in-Publication Data

Names: Winn, Kevin P., author. | Wing, Kelisa, author.
Title: Atrocities in action / Kevin P. Winn, Kelisa Wing.
Description: Ann Arbor, Michigan : Cherry Lake Publishing, [2022] | Series:
Racial justice in America: histories | Includes index. | Audience: Grades: 4-6 | Summary: "The Racial Justice in America:
   Histories series explores moments and eras in America's history that have been ignored or misrepresented in education due
   to racial bias. Atrocities in Action explores the various forms of violent and cruel oppression Black people have endured over
   the years in a comprehensive, honest, and age-appropriate way. Developed in conjunction with educator, advocate, and
   author Kelisa Wing to reach children of all races and encourage them to approach our history with open eyes and minds. Books
   include 21st Century Skills and content, as well as activities created by Wing. Also includes a table of contents, glossary,
   index, author biography, sidebars, educational matter, and activities"— Provided by publisher.
Identifiers: LCCN 2021010808 (print) | LCCN 2021010809 (ebook) | ISBN 9781534187498 (hardcover)
   | ISBN 9781534188891 (paperback) | ISBN 9781534190290 (pdf) | ISBN 9781534191693 (ebook)
Subjects: LCSH: African Americans—Violence against—History—Juvenile literature. | Lynching—United States— History—Juvenile
   literature. | Racism—United States—Juvenile literature. | United States—Race relations— Juvenile literature.
Classification: LCC E185 .W767 2022 (print) | LCC E185 (ebook) | DDC 305.800973—dc23
LC record available at https://lccn.loc.gov/2021010808
LC ebook record available at https://lccn.loc.gov/2021010809

Cherry Lake Publishing Group would like to acknowledge the work of the Partnership for 21st Century Learning, a Network of Battelle for Kids. Please visit *http://www.battelleforkids.org/networks/p21* for more information.

Printed in the United States of America

Kevin P. Winn is a children's book writer and researcher. He focuses on issues of racial justice and educational equity in his work. In 2020, Kevin earned his doctorate in Educational Policy and Evaluation from Arizona State University.

Kelisa Wing honorably served in the U.S. Army and has been an educator for 14 years. She is the author of *Promises and Possibilities: Dismantling the School to Prison Pipeline, If I Could: Lessons for Navigating an Unjust World*, and *Weeds & Seeds: How to Stay Positive in the Midst of Life's Storms*. She speaks both nationally and internationally about discipline reform, equity, and student engagement. Kelisa lives in Northern Virginia with her husband and two children.

Chapter 1

What Is an Atrocity? | Page 4

Chapter 2

Lynching in Early U.S. History | Page 8

Chapter 3

The Rise of White Terrorism | Page 12

Chapter 4

Lynching in Plain View | Page 16

Chapter 5

Targeting Veterans | Page 22

Chapter 6

Unpunished Crimes and Lynching's Legacy | Page 26

SHOW WHAT YOU KNOW | Page 31

Extend Your Learning | Page 32

Glossary | Page 32

Index | Page 32

CHAPTER 1

What Is an Atrocity?

Have you ever been treated extremely cruelly? How did that make you feel? What if that treatment continued for years upon years? Throughout U.S. history, people of color have faced—and continue to face—violence because of their skin color. This is an atrocity. In particular, Black people have suffered in this country because of slavery.

People from the United States and Europe kidnapped Africans from their homes. Africans were then sold and forced to work on plantations owned by White people. White landowners did not pay enslaved people. They also treated them harshly. As slavery continued through the 1860s, plantation owners in the Southern states punished enslaved people by torturing and sometimes murdering them. They also separated families, selling them to different slave owners. Sometimes, family members never saw each other again.

In 1863, President Abraham Lincoln issued the Emancipation Proclamation, which freed enslaved people in the Southern states that had left the Union. White slave owners ignored this proclamation. They didn't believe Black people deserved freedom. They worked hard to keep control over Black people. One way they did this was through racial terror lynchings.

Although the Emancipation Proclamation made slavery illegal, the United States passed the Thirteenth Amendment to end slavery through the U.S. Constitution. But some states didn't ratify the Thirteenth Amendment until much later. Kentucky ratified it in 1976 and Mississippi in 1995—more than 100 years after slavery had ended.

A racial terror lynching is a type of violence where a mob of people take the law into their own hands. Often, they murder a Black person in brutal and public ways. Many racial terror lynchings ended with hanging the victim in a public place. In most racial terror lynchings, mobs of White people attacked and killed Black people because of their skin color. White people made excuses, claiming they had real reasons to kill their victims. But historians have proved that White people made up many of these stories. Black people were blamed for crimes they didn't do. Because of the fear that anyone could be the next victim of a racial terror lynching, White people controlled the movements of Black people. When Black people spoke against a lynching, they became the next target. Few Black people said anything because they were scared they would be killed.

Many racial terror lynchings were never recorded. However, historians know that between 1877 and 1950, White people lynched at least 4,084 Black people. The actual number is probably much higher.

The National Memorial for Peace and Justice in Alabama opened in 2018 as a space for visitors to reflect on America's history of racial injustice and violence.

CHAPTER 2

Lynching in Early U.S. History

When the Civil War ended in 1865, an era called Reconstruction began. During this time, the U.S. government helped rebuild the South, which had committed treason against the United States during the Civil War. Eleven Southern states had left the United States to form their own government because White people in those states didn't want to abolish slavery. Lynchings became popular during this time.

Only a year after the Civil War ended, U.S. President Andrew Johnson forgave many of the people in the South. He also supported laws making it hard for formerly enslaved people to buy land. White landowners in the South saw Johnson as a friend. They knew he wouldn't enforce the Thirteenth Amendment.

Many people in the Southern states didn't like Reconstruction because they didn't want to elevate the status of Black people living there.

White people worked to terrorize Black people through violence during Andrew Johnson's presidency. In 1866, attacks by White police officers and White mobs in Memphis, Tennessee, and New Orleans, Louisiana, left almost 100 Black people dead and hundreds injured.

A scene from Memphis, Tennessee, during the 1866 race riot

Reconstruction lasted only until 1877. As the U.S. government made little effort to protect formerly enslaved people—and Black people in general—White people in the South re-established their power. They claimed they were superior to Black people. White people did this through terrorizing Black people by threatening them with lynchings.

With the passage of the Thirteenth, Fourteenth, and Fifteenth Amendments, Black people gained freedoms and rights. In fact, Black people began making more money and started successful businesses. As Black people's power grew, Southern White people felt threatened. They worked together to stop Black success, claiming that they would put Black people "in their place."

The Civil War Amendments granted Black people legal rights in the United States. The Thirteenth abolished slavery, the Fourteenth gave citizenship to people born or **naturalized** in the United States, and the Fifteenth allowed people the right to vote.

CHAPTER 3

The Rise of White Terrorism

After the Civil War, White people formed a terrorist organization called the Ku Klux Klan (KKK). Its purpose was to spread White supremacy—a belief that White people should rule over everyone. The KKK spread around the country but was mostly located in the South. Many White people joined, including city mayors, police officers, doctors, and lawyers. Because White people in powerful positions were part of this group, they didn't get in trouble for racial terror lynchings.

Not only did police allow lynchings in the South, but some also joined in the violence. They sometimes helped other White people murder Black people. They didn't punish members of lynch mobs.

Chapters of the KKK existed, and still exist, all over the United States. The group above was based in Watertown, New York.

KKK members wore hooded white robes for ceremonies and acts of violence. They also burned crosses.

White terrorism existed along with Jim Crow segregation in the Southern United States. Under Jim Crow laws, Black and White people remained separated in most parts of life. Black people had to use separate bathrooms. They had to enter different doors to theaters and other buildings. People of different races couldn't marry or have meaningful relationships with one another. When Black people broke these laws—or were suspected of doing so—they faced the real fear of White mobs lynching them.

In Tennessee in 1901, a Black man found a wallet and kept the money in it. A White mob captured him for this, but he escaped. Instead, the mob lynched the man's sister, Ballie Crutchfield. She hadn't had anything to do with the wallet incident.

CHAPTER 4

Lynching in Plain View

What made lynching particularly cruel and terrifying was how public it was. Throughout the history of racial terror lynching, White people made no effort to hide their involvement. This fact made it even scarier for Black people. They knew White lynchers wouldn't be punished for murdering their friends and family members.

Lynchings didn't just take place under the cover of night. Many times, they happened during the day in public areas for entire communities to view. In fact, some newspapers at the time published articles with headlines saying a Black person would be lynched that day. They did this so that White people could come and watch.

Racial terror lynchings were often meant to be public events.

When White people learned about an upcoming lynching, they treated it like a party. Thousands of White people—including children—gathered. Bringing picnic lunches with them, they ate as they watched White friends and neighbors torture Black people. After the lynching, spectators would sometimes take "souvenirs," including bits of the rope used to hang the murdered Black person. Others made postcards to remember the event.

Newspapers owned by White people printed lies about Black people, but White people believed them. Newspapers blamed Black people for crimes they hadn't done. White mobs formed to lynch innocent Black people before Black people could tell their side of the story.

A group of White people watch a lynching of two Black men in Indiana in 1930.

Many Black families were run out of entire neighborhoods and communities across the South.

White people were creative in their cruel efforts to scare Black people. To warn Black people not to question their rules, White people made Black people watch lynchings. After a lynching, mobs often brought their victim into neighborhoods where Black people lived. They then further defiled the body in truly shocking ways. After doing this, White mobs warned Black people that they weren't welcome in town. If they didn't leave, they would be the next victim.

The effects of racial terror lynchings linger today. As of 2020, some communities in the South have almost no Black residents. This is because Black people were once threatened with lynching if they didn't leave. Black people never returned to live in these towns.

CHAPTER 5

Targeting Veterans

Black veterans of wars have been especially targeted for lynchings. Although 200,000 Black Americans served in the U.S. military during World War I and 1.2 million served in World War II, their willingness to die for their country hasn't been appreciated.

Many Black people thought their military service would be rewarded when they returned to the United States. They believed that because the United States was fighting to spread democracy around the world, they would be treated as human beings with rights. This turned out to be wrong. Instead, White people saw soldiers as threats. They lynched 13 Black veterans after WWI.

Hosea Williams, a veteran and civil rights leader, once said, "I had fought in WWII, and I once was captured by the German army, and I want to tell you the Germans never were as inhumane as the state troopers in Alabama."

Hosea Williams (right) and John Lewis were leaders of the civil rights movement in the United States.

White people believed that Black veterans challenged White supremacy in the South. They thought Black people would want more power and rights—which they did—after fighting in the wars. But it wasn't just Southerners who believed this. White veterans received generous amounts of money from the G.I. Bill after WWII, which helped them get money for education, housing, and businesses. However, Black veterans almost never got this money. This showed that many White people didn't value Black veterans' service to the country.

Black veterans were blamed for the mistreatment they faced from White people. Even when Black people were attacked, White people accused the victims. For example, three masked men attacked Johnson C. Whittaker, one of the first Black people to attend West Point Military Academy, in his dorm room. The men beat him, broke his nose, and tied him to his bed. After Whitaker was discovered, West Point officials kicked him out of school. They claimed he had made up the entire story.

During a summer of violence in 1919, Black people fought back. They challenged the White mobs who started racist violence against them. After fighting for democracy in Europe, they fought for democracy in their home country.

More than one million Black men registered for military service during World War II.

CHAPTER 6

Unpunished Crimes and Lynching's Legacy

White people who lynched Black people were not often punished. Participants in only 1 percent of all lynchings since 1900 were convicted of a crime. Even with evidence against them—including witnesses and pictures—White lynchers walked free.

Many Black people felt powerless because they had no place to report the crimes committed against them. They couldn't trust the police, who often participated in lynch mobs. However, one brave Black woman named Ida B. Wells decided to investigate lynchings and hold White people accountable. She traveled around the South and reported on lynchings, even when White Southerners threatened to murder her. The efforts she made brought attention to lynchings for the first time. Much of our knowledge about racial terror lynchings in the early 1900s is due to her courage.

Ida B. Wells was also one of the founders of the National Association for the Advancement of Colored People (NAACP).

Capital punishment and police brutality is one way the legacy of lynchings continues in the United States.

Americans have a history of claiming to have solved problems and saying they are issues of the past. However, the country also has a history of simply changing the name of these problems but not actually fixing the issue. This has happened with lynching.

Historians explain that starting in the 1920s, lynchings in the South made these states look bad. So, instead, the South passed laws to encourage capital punishment. Capital punishment remains a part of the law in 28 states in the United States. Black people are the most likely to be punished in this way. Black people make up 13.4 percent of the U.S. population. However, they make up 41.38 percent of those on death row.

The Equal Justice Initiative (EJI) is working to bring attention to the victims of lynchings. Their work helps tell the hidden histories of many Black people who were murdered. In 2018, the EJI opened the National Memorial for Peace and Justice and the Legacy Museum: From Enslavement to Mass Incarceration in Montgomery, Alabama. This memorial remembers and honors the victims of slavery, racial terror lynchings, and mass incarceration. The memorial is important because it documents America's racist past. It is located in Alabama, where slavery was widespread. The state also has one of the most violent histories of racism.

Activists have recognized that Black people still get punished for crimes at unfair rates compared to White people. They are working to outlaw capital punishment throughout the United States.

SHOW WHAT YOU KNOW

An atrocity is an extremely wicked or cruel act, typically one involving physical violence or injury. The mistreatment described in this book discusses many of the atrocities Black people, including military veterans, have suffered. In spite of all of this, Black people have kept going in the face of hardship.

In 1966, Gary Steele became the first Black varsity football player at West Point Military Academy. In 2008, Barack Obama became the first Black person to serve as president of the United States. In 2017, Simone Askew became the first Black woman to be named the first captain of cadets at West Point. On January 20, 2021, Kamala Harris became the 46th vice president of the United States. She is the first Black person and first woman to have the job. There are so many other people who, despite major atrocities in America, have continued to push forward.

For this project, research someone in the past or present who has accomplished something great in challenging times.

Do you know there are so many different ways to show what you know? Rather than using traditional ways to display knowledge, try something new to complete this assignment. Here are some ideas:

1. Rap
2. Mural
3. Musical
4. Debate
5. Web page
6. Speech
7. Bulletin board
8. Jigsaw puzzle
9. Show and tell
10. Essay
11. Diorama
12. Performance
13. Podcast
14. Journal
15. OR add your own...

EXTEND YOUR LEARNING

Jenn M. Jackson, "Lynching in the United States, Explained," *Teen Vogue*, October 2, 2017, www.teenvogue.com/story/lynching-in-the-united-states-explained. Accessed February 1, 2021.

Legacy Museum and National Memorial for Peace and Justice
museumandmemorial.eji.org

GLOSSARY

abolish (uh-BOL-ish) to end something officially

atrocity (uh-TRAW-suh-tee) a shockingly horrible act or situation

capital punishment (kap-UH-tuhl PUH-nish-muhnt) the practice of killing people for a crime that they are believed to be guilty of

death row (DETH ROH) the area of a prison where people who are sentenced to death live

defiled (dih-FYLD) treated with great disrespect or dishonor

democracy (dih-MOK-ruh-see) a form of government where citizens elect people to represent them to make laws

enforce (in-FORSS) to make someone follow a rule or law

inhumane (in-HYOO-mayne) something that is cruel; inhumane treatment is treating someone like they aren't human

Jim Crow segregation (JIHM CROH seg-ruh-GAY-shuhn) a system of laws that separated White people from other races, especially Black people

mass incarceration (MASS in-kahr-suh-RAY-shuhn) the process by which the United States imprisons its people at high rates

naturalized (NAH-chuh-ruh-lyzd) a person who is allowed to become a citizen

plantations (plan-TAY-shuhns) large farms that used enslaved people to do their work

racial terror lynchings (RAY-shuhl TER-uhr LINCH-ings) violent attacks by White people on BIPOC, especially Black people, to scare and control them; usually done through torture, murder, and hanging

ratify (RAH-tuh-feye) to officially approve of something, such as a law

spectators (SPEK-tay-turs) people who watch something

treason (TREE-zuhn) betraying your own country

White supremacy (WITE suh-PREH-muh-see) the incorrect belief that White people and their ideas are superior to all others

INDEX

Alabama, 7, 23, 30
Askew, Simone, 31
atrocities
  what they are, 4–7

Black people, 4, 6
  after Reconstruction era, 11
  and capital punishment, 29, 30
  and racial terror lynchings,
    5–6, 10
  unpunished crimes against,
    26–30
  veterans as targets of
    lynchings, 22–25

capital punishment, 29, 30
Civil War, 8
Civil War Amendments, 11
crimes, unpunished, 26–30
cruelty, 4

death row, 29

Emancipation Proclamation, 5
enslaved people, 4–5, 8, 11
Equal Justice Initiative (EJI), 30

Fifteenth Amendment, 11
Fourteenth Amendment, 11
freedoms, 5, 11

G.I. Bill, 24
Gordon, Fred A., 31

hangings, 6
Harris, Kamala, 31

Jim Crow segregation, 15
Johnson, Andrew, 8, 10

Ku Klux Klan (KKK), 12–15

Legacy Museum, 30
Lewis, John, 23
Lincoln, Abraham, 5
lynchings, 5–6, 11, 12, 15
  and Black veterans, 22–25
  in early U.S. history, 8–11
  and Ida B. Wells, 26–27
  legacy of, 21, 26–30
  role of newspapers in, 18
  visibility of, 16–21

Memphis, TN, 10
military service, 22–25
mobs, 6, 10, 25
Montgomery, AL, 7, 30
murder, 6, 12, 16

National Memorial for Peace and
  Justice, 7, 30
New Orleans, LA, 10
newspapers, 18

Obama, Barack, 31

plantations, 4–5
police, 12

racial terror lynchings. *See*
  lynchings
Reconstruction era, 8, 11

segregation, 15
slavery, 4, 5, 8, 11
Southern states, 4, 8
  and Ku Klux Klan, 12–15
  and lynchings, 29
Steele, Gary, 31

terrorism, White, 12–15
Thirteenth Amendment, 5, 8, 11
treason, 8

veterans, Black, 22–25
violence, 4, 6, 10, 12, 25

Wells, Ida B., 26–27
West Point Military Academy, 24,
  31
White people, 4–5
  and racial terror lynchings, 6,
    10, 21
  try to stop Black success after
    Civil War, 11
  unpunished for lynchings,
    26–30
  view lynchings as party, 18
White supremacy, 11, 12–15, 24
Whittaker, Johnson C., 24
Williams, Darryl, 31
Williams, Hosea, 23